I Am Blind

Julie Haydon

Contents

Rigby®

A Harcourt Achieve Imprint

www.Rigby.com
1-800-531-5015

I Am Blind

You see with your eyes.

You can see your mom
and dad and your friends.

You can see many things.

I cannot see.
I am blind.

Reading

I cannot read
with my eyes.
But I can read
with my fingers.

Look at the dots
on this page.
The dots make words.

On Friday
the fifth egg
cracked
and out came
a baby
turtle.

Writing

I write the dots

on some paper at school.

My teacher helps me.

I can write like this, too.

This computer can talk.

I write the words.
The computer
says the words
back to me.

9

My Watch

This is my watch.

It can talk.

I push a button.

My watch tells me the time.

My Books

I have some books
that talk, too.
I can hear the story.

My Cane

I have a **cane**.

I tap the ground
with my cane.
My cane helps me
to feel things
that are in my way.

Dad's Guide Dog

My dad is blind, too.

Dad has a **guide dog**.

The dog can see.

Dad's guide dog helps him to walk around safely.

Glossary

cane

guide dog